A Message to Parents, Teachers, and Other Caring Adults

Imagine going to a social event. You show up in shorts and a T-shirt, thinking it's a picnic, and it turns out to be a black-tie affair. You feel so different, and for those few hours you can think of nothing else.

Children may feel different for many reasons. Some of the reasons are important, and some of them seem trivial. Some of the reasons are obvious. Others are held only in the child's heart.

In every case, the child needs to know that the feeling is real. We can't shrug it off and say, "You're being silly" or "You'll grow out of it." The child needs to know that the emotion—and the child him- or herself for feeling it—is not bad or stupid.

Children need honesty. Saying "No one will notice" or "No one really cares" will feel like a lie to them. Ignoring the matter can be as hurtful as overemphasizing it. Either can make the child feel as if the difference is a cause for shame.

The best way to strike a balance is to surround the child with love. Children need to be loved just because they are. They also need to be told—*out loud*—how much they're loved. We adults are used to dealing with unspoken feelings. Children do not have the ability to "read" this hidden language. Every day they need to hear the words and to feel the hugs.

When children have been strengthened by love, it is easier for them to see that differences are just a very small part of who they are. Children rooted in love are also secure enough to reach out to others in *their* differences. And they are able to offer the world all the gifts and talents that make them who they truly are.

—Susan Heyboer O'Keefe

You're Different!

No one in the world is exactly like you!

Being different seems like a good thing if you're smart or funny, very strong or very brave, a champion speller or a prize-winning artist. Your talents and gifts are part of what makes you the special person you are.

But sometimes you may not be as smart or as funny, as strong or as brave as other people. Or you may even feel "too smart" or "too funny." That may make you feel different in a way that feels bad.

Be the Star That You Are!

A Book for Kids Who Feel Different

Written by
Susan Heyboer O'Keefe

Illustrated by
R. W. Alley

Abbey Press
St. Meinrad, IN 47577

For Michael and Daniel

Text © 2005 Susan Heyboer O'Keefe
Illustrations © 2005 St. Meinrad Archabbey
Published by One Caring Place
Abbey Press
St. Meinrad, Indiana 47577

Library of Congress Catalog Number
2004097520

ISBN 0-87029-391-5

Printed in the United States of America

Different on the Outside

You may think you're too fat or too thin, too tall or too short. You may think you have too many freckles, that your ears are too big, or that your hair is too kinky.

This is like saying that stripes are too straight, or that polka dots are too round! You're really not TOO anything. You're just you, and this is just how *you* look. Right now, you look one way. When you are older, you may look another way.

Ask some grownups to show you pictures of themselves when they were your age. You'll be surprised at how they have changed over the years! You will change too.

A Secret Superhero

Imagine how a big toe feels. It's fat and stumpy. Sometimes it sweats and stinks a little. It's not pretty like hair or bright like eyes. It doesn't get to hear music or to taste delicious food. No one will ever say, "What a wonderful, beautiful, clever big toe!"

But without a big toe, you couldn't run. You would even have problems walking. A big toe is very important! It's like a secret superhero.

Being stumpy or stinky isn't bad. It's just the way the big toe is. And that doesn't change how important it is.

Looking Different

There are other ways of looking different that may make you feel different in a bad way.

A part of your body may need help for a while—like braces for your teeth or a wig for your head. It may need help forever—like eyeglasses or an inhaler or a wheelchair.

But *you* are not your hair. You are not your legs. You are so much more—more than you can ever imagine! Adding up all your separate parts still wouldn't equal YOU.

A World of Differences

Maybe you don't look like other kids you know. Maybe you come from far away and speak a different language, eat different foods, wear different clothes, and say different prayers.

All these differences—and many more—are just some of the things that make you one of a kind, and that's a very good thing.

Which makes a better picture? Coloring with one crayon or with many crayons? To create the world, God used the jumbo box of crayons— every single one!

Different on the Inside

Maybe you don't *look* different on the outside. Maybe you *feel* different on the inside—stupid or clumsy, always wrong, or good at nothing!

You may not be as smart or as graceful as others. But there are things that you *can* do, and things that you *like* to do. Even if you make a mistake, and even if kids laugh, you have the right to try! How will you know what you like and what you're good at if you don't try things?

Talent is not always a tall tree in the middle of an empty field, easy to spot from far away. Sometimes talent is like gold, and you have to dig long and hard like a miner to find it.

Hidden Treasure

Even if you know what you're good at, you may be too shy to let people know. You may not be able to make friends easily. You may not raise your hand in class. You may not even tell your own family what's going on inside you.

Your parents want to know how you feel, so try extra hard to talk with them. Tell them you have something very important to say. That way, they will stop and pay special attention.

You are a treasure, but sometimes you have to give people a map so they can discover the real you.

The Gift of You

When you feel different, you may think no one likes you. Other people are more popular. Other people get chosen for teams. Other people have more friends.

You may begin to think it's somehow your fault and wonder, "Why can't I be like everyone else?"

You are a gift from God. Imagine if you went to a party and everyone brought the same gift—bunny slippers. The birthday child might like bunny slippers. But twenty-two pairs?

God wanted to give lots of different gifts to the world! God wanted one exactly like *you*.

X-ray Vision

Sometimes kids make fun of other kids who seem different. They may call them names or not play with them.

If this has ever happened to you, it surely hurt your feelings. But it doesn't mean there's anything wrong with you.

Some people act like this because they don't look past the outside of you. They don't see who you really are on the inside.

Other people have a kind of "X-ray vision." They can look into your heart and see the goodness there. Practice using X-ray vision, and other kids might learn it too!

Be a Friend

From time to time, you may see that look of "feeling different" on someone else's face.

That is a good time for you to be a friend, even if you just say hello. Soon, someone may see when *you* are feeling different, and be your friend.

We are all people. We are all connected to each other because we are more alike than we are different.

You're Not Alone

You'd be surprised to find out how many people feel different. On the outside, they seem to be the fastest and the strongest. But sometimes they feel alone, or afraid, or weird. Their reason may not be the same as yours, but the *feeling* of being different is the same.

We often think that everyone else notices everything that is wrong with us, just the way we do. But here's a secret: Other people are often so worried about how different THEY feel, they never even notice what's different about you.

Only You

What are *your* special talents, the things that make you special?

Well, what do you do best? Sing, tell jokes, do math, juggle, cook, fix things, draw? Maybe you give great hugs. Or you know how to be a good friend.

Maybe everything that has happened to you in your life has taught you to be very understanding. Now you are teaching it to others just by being yourself.

Different People and Gifts

Many people—each one different—mean many different gifts.

It's wonderful to be a great painter. But what if everyone in the world were a great painter? Who would make the paints? And who would make the brushes? Painting is hard work! Who would grow the food, build the beds, and sew the clothes for all those hungry, tired, cold painters?

No matter what special gifts you have, they are important!

Let Your Light Shine!

God made only one of you, and you are perfect just as you are. How you look, how you move, how you think—everything about you is just right.

You are a gift—all of you, all by yourself, even when you're sound asleep. Your family and friends love you. God loves you, too, right now, just as you are.

You have everything you need to be the person God wants you to be. So be different, be proud, and shine like the star you are!

Susan Heyboer O'Keefe is the author of many books for children, including the best-selling picture book *One Hungry Monster* (with more Hungry Monster books on the way); a middle-grade comedy, *Death by Eggplant*; and a teen mystery, *My Life and Death by Alexandra Canarsie*. Her books for Catholic kids include *What Does a Priest Do? / What Does a Nun Do?* and *It's Great to Be Catholic!* She lives in New Jersey with her husband, son, and two parrots.

R. W. Alley is the illustrator for the popular Abbey Press adult series of Elf-help books, as well as an illustrator and writer of children's books. He lives in Barrington, Rhode Island, with his wife, daughter, and son.